A .HELEN EX

granama

PICTURES BY JOANNA KIDNEY

A grandmother always
has time for you
when the rest of the world
is busy.

AUTHOR UNKNOWN

GRANDMA ALWAYS
MAKES YOU FEEL
SHE HAS BEEN WAITING
TO SEE JUST YOU
ALL DAY
AND NOW THE DAY
IS COMPLETE.

MARCY DE MARREE

I accepted her presence
in my life
as if she were
a great protective tree.

M.F.K. FISHER (1908–1992),
FROM "TO BEGIN AGAIN"

...grandparents are in a unique position
to provide some of the things
that money just can't buy:
continuity, trust, stability, love,
understanding,
and unconditional support.

DR. RUTH K. WESTHEIMER AND STEVE KAPLAN,
FROM "GRANDPARENTHOOD"

Grandparents somehow sprinkle

a sense of stardust
over grandchildren.

ALEX HALEY (1921–1992)

Grandmothers
come in dozens of ages, shapes,
bunches of wrinkles, languages,
clothes and skins.
But they all have exactly
the same love in the middle.

PAM BROWN, B.1928

Grandmother and grandchild

discussing a common interest
are exactly the same age.

DUANE BIRCH

Far-away grans have learned to

send love down the telephone.

RENE JEAN HESSE

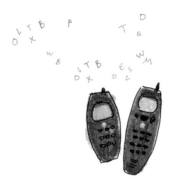

Grandma was a kind of a first-aid station...
who took up where the battle ended,
accepting us
and our little sobbing sins,
gathering the whole of us into her lap,
restoring us to health
and confidence....

LILLIAN SMITH,
FROM "MOTHER TO DAUGHTER,
DAUGHTER TO MOTHER"

Grandmothers hold families together,
stitching the rents that come with time,
darning the weak,
sponging out spots and stains,
starching new strength into worn fabric.

PAM BROWN, B.1928

When it seems
the world can't understand,
Your grandmother's there
to hold your hand.

JOYCE K. ALLEN LOGAN

Every Saturday I visit my granny
and we discuss what we did during the week.
I talk to her about everything,
she understands me.
When I am sad she cheers me up
and we laugh together.

MARIA FEENEY, AGE 9,
FROM "TO THE WORLD'S BEST GRANDMA"

She always says who is this big boy
and she measures me on a bit of paper.
Then we have a cup of tea
and bread and buns.
Just the two of us.

BARRY O'CALLAGHAN, AGE 7

Most grandmas have
a touch of the scallywag about them.
And from the very beginning,
their grandchildren know it!

HELEN THOMSON

GRANDCHILDREN ARE
THE BEST EXCUSE
GRANDMOTHERS HAVE
TO DO ALL
THE UNDIGNIFIED THINGS
THAT ARE SO
MUCH FUN.

MARION C. GARRETTY

Grandmas don't just say "that's nice"
  – they reel back
              and roll their eyes
  and throw up their hands and smile.
  You get your money's worth
                out of grandmas.

PAM BROWN, B.1928

Grandmothers come to call
carrying big bags
with Very Interesting Bulges.

PAM BROWN, B.1928

My Nana always seems
to have a little tuck shop
at the bottom of her bag.

FIONA WALKER, AGE 10

A grandma is just a teenager

with many years of experience.

STUART & LINDA MACFARLANE

Grandmothers put
things up in jars....
For days the kitchen is
given over to the making of chutney
and pervaded by an extensive
inventory of delightful
and mysterious smells.

PAGE SMITH,
FROM "OLD AGE IS ANOTHER COUNTRY"

When she squeezed me,
I felt like a tube of toothpaste.
...I felt as if
all my insides would come out.
She had a joyous, happy laugh
that started way down inside her
and rolled out.

RORY ELDER, CHOCTOW,
FROM "TURN THE OTHER CHEEK"

"I cultivate Being Uppity.
It's something
     My Gramom taught me."

KATE RUSHIN, FROM "FAMILY TREE"

There's a quiet place, with Grandma,
where we can all find
a little peace
when our lives get
too busy and too loud.

PAM BROWN, B.1928

For a child, a grandmother
with a stock of rhymes
        and songs and stories
is the opener of doors
    – to plays and poetry, music,
            myth and magic.
To places far away
        and long ago.

CHARLOTTE GRAY, B.1937

Grandmothers are...
the memory banks,
the recorders of birthdays, anniversaries,
of addresses and phone numbers...
and all the things
that make it possible
for life to go on from day to day.

PAGE SMITH,
FROM "OLD AGE IS ANOTHER COUNTRY"

I love to hold your hands,
Grandma.
They lead me back to the time
before I began.
They keep me safe
against the world outside.
They reassure me
that I am worth a lot.

PAMELA DUGDALE

Although it's not always practical,
I love taking Grandma on tour
as she acts as a good luck charm;
she has this knack
of exerting a calming influence
on all who come into
contact with her.

VANESSA–MAE, VIOLINIST, B.1978,
FROM "HELLO MAGAZINE", FEBRUARY 14, 1998

We danced on and on,
unequal partners who
in those moments absolutely loved
all the inequalities about us....
My grandmother was singing:
her voice was loud and clear.
She spun me for a long time.
Our heads thrown back....

MARCIE HERSHMAN

At once indomitable,
somehow timeless,
able to span the generations;
wise, loving, and an utterly irresistible
mischievousness of spirit.

H.R.H. THE PRINCE OF WALES'S TRIBUTE
TO HIS GRANDMOTHER

My grandmother has...
helped me to choose [my] direction...
My debt to her is to succeed
in achieving goals
she believes I can attain.

KHAYA, FROM "REMEMBRANCES"

Grandmother preserves and maintains
her culture for all her people
by bridging the gap
between past and present....
Infusing daily life for her family and friends
with the timeless essence of tradition....

JAN REYNOLDS,
FROM "MOTHER AND CHILD"

She is more
than my grandma,
she is
my friend.

NICOLA THOMIS, AGE 10

Grandmothers are in a position
to say, "Never Mind, Love.
It will pass. Truly."

PAM BROWN, B.1928

Grandmothers are very good
at picking up the pieces of something
shattered beyond all mending
— and mending it.

CLARA ORTEGA, B.1955

The best present you ever gave me
was your kindness.
No grandma could ever match
your kind heart.
I appreciate everything you give me.

AARON MCCULLOUGH, AGE 10,
FROM "TO THE WORLD'S BEST GRANDMA"

She and I are very close.
We are so in tune that we always know
if something is making the other
happy or unhappy.

VANESSA-MAE, VIOLINIST, B.1978,
FROM "HELLO MAGAZINE", FEBRUARY 14, 1998

She gave me what many people do not gain in an entire lifetime. What I owe my grandmother, I think I could never repay.

KHAYA, FROM "REMEMBRANCES"

A grandmother would like

to take you everywhere – but…

accepts that you will

make your own way

to Paris

and Istanbul and China.

But think of her

when you get there.

Her spirit will be with you.

PAM BROWN, B.1928

For all the ordinary, happy things
you've put aside to care for us;
for all the hope and courage
you've instilled; for all your patience.
Thank you.

CHARLOTTE GRAY, B.1937

Thank you for showing me
that I'm vital to the human race.
Thank you for showing me
that everyone
in the whole world is related.
Thank you for being my grandma.

PAM BROWN, B.1928

My "good old days" are being

created by what we do today,
Grandma and me.

DOUGLAS MCLEAN

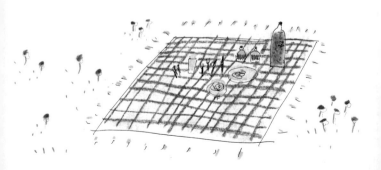

GRANDMOTHERS ARE VERY IMPORTANT.
GRANDMOTHERS ARE THE HUB
OF THE SACRED HOOP.
THEY ARE BEACONS OF LIGHT
SAYING,
"THIS IS WHERE YOU ARE GOING."

MAHISHA

I basked in her love as

in the warmth of a private sun.

JOYCE CAROL OATES, B.1938,
FROM "WHY DONT YOU COME LIVE WITH ME
IT'S TIME"

I'll never forget those memories.
They will remain as vivid to me
as the day we made them.
I will cherish them always.

SIÁN E. MORGAN, B.1973

As a grandmother
you are special to your grandchild
as no one else can be.

DR. JOAN GOMEZ,
FROM "YOU AND YOUR GRANDCHILD"

Grandmas hold
a place in your heart forever.

PAM BROWN, B.1928

Helen Exley runs her own publishing company which sells giftbooks in more than seventy countries. She had always wanted to do a little book on smiles, and had been collecting the quotations for many years, but always felt that the available illustrations just weren't quite right. Helen fell in love with Joanna Kidney's happy, bright pictures and knew immediately they had the feel she was looking for. She asked Joanna to work on *smile*, and then to go on to contribute the art for four more books: *friend, happy day!, love* and *hope! dream!* We have now published nine more books in this series, which are selling in 27 languages.

Joanna Kidney lives in County Wicklow in Ireland. She juggles her time between working on various illustration projects, producing her own art for shows and exhibitions and looking after her baby boy. Her whole range of greeting cards, *Joanna's Pearlies* – some of which appear in this book – won the prestigious Henries oscar for 'best fun or graphic range'.